The Gospel
of
John
made easy

Mark Water

D0840023

HENDRICKSON
PUBLISHERS

The Gospel of John Made Easy
Hendrickson Publishers, Inc.
P.O. Box 3473
Peabody, Massachusetts 01961-3473

Copyright © 2000 John Hunt Publishing Ltd
Text copyright © 2000 Mark Water

ISBN 1-56563-526-4

Original edition published
in English under the title
"The Gospel of John made easy"
by John Hunt Publishing Ltd,
Alresford, Hants, UK.

Designed and produced
by Tony Cantale Graphics

First printing – September 2000

Manufactured in Hong Kong/China

Photography supplied by Artville
Digital Vision, Foxx Photos,
Goodshoot, PhotoAlto,
Photodisc and Tony Cantale

Illustrations by
Tony Cantale Graphics

CONTENTS

SPECIAL PULL-OUT CHART

John's Gospel: an extended outline and reading plan

FACT FILE:
JOHN'S GOSPEL

WHO WROTE THIS GOSPEL?

John. That is, John, the brother of James. He also wrote three letters in the New Testament, 1 John, 2 John, 3 John, as well as the book of Revelation.

Pointers to John's authorship

- John is prominent in the other Gospels, but is not named in this one.
- The Gospel was written by "the disciple whom Jesus loved." *21:20.* This person may be identified as John. "This is the disciple who testifies to these things and who wrote them down." *21:24*
- Early writers such as Irenaeus and Tertullian were certain that John wrote this Gospel.

JOHN WAS WELL-SITUATED TO WRITE A GOSPEL

1. With Peter and James, John was one of the inner three of Jesus' disciples, who witnessed:
   - Jairus' daughter being brought to life,
   - Jesus' transfiguration, and
   - was close to Jesus as he prayed in the Garden of Gethsemane. *See Luke 8:51; Matthew 17:1; Mark 14:33.*
2. With Peter, he was entrusted with the task of preparing the Last Supper. *See Luke 22:7.*
3. He was at Jesus' side during the Last Supper. *13:23*
4. Jesus asked John to look after his mother, Mary. *19:26-27*
5. John was the first disciple to believe in Jesus' resurrection. *20:8*
6. John was the first disciple to recognize the risen Jesus on the shore of Galilee. *21:7*

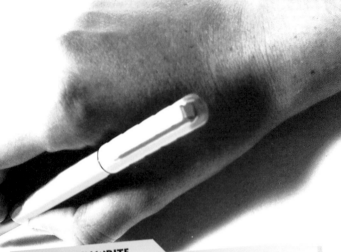

WHY DID JOHN WRITE HIS GOSPEL?

We are not left in doubt about why John wrote this book. Unlike Matthew, Mark and Luke, John spells out the purpose behind his writing. He wrote so his readers might "believe that Jesus is the Christ."

"Jesus did many other miraculous signs in the presence of his disciples, which are not recorded in this book. But these are written that you may believe that Jesus is the Christ, the Son of God, and that by believing you may have life in his name." 20:30-31

Everlasting life is one of the key themes in this Gospel.

JOHN'S BACKGROUND
- A fisherman in partnership with his brother and Peter. *Matthew 4:21-22; Luke 5:10-11*
- A person of means who owned his own home and hired servants. *John 19:27; Mark 1:19-20*
- He knew the high priest at Jerusalem well enough to be present at Jesus' trial before Anna and Caiaphas. *John 18:12-16*

OVERVIEW:
JOHN'S GOSPEL

A BIRD'S EYE VIEW

Introduction	1:1–51
Public ministry of the Son of God	2:1–12:50
Private ministry of the Son of God	13:1–17:26
Death and resurrection of the Son of God	18:1–20:31
Epilogue	21:1-25

KEY WORD
Belief

The key word in John's Gospel is "belief" or "faith". These two words and related words occur over 100 times in John's Gospel. Looking up these words in John's Gospel reveals:

- The characteristics of Christian belief
- How this faith should be expressed
- What we receive from believing in Jesus

OTHER KEY WORDS

Besides "belief," and related words which appear over 100 times in John's Gospel, there are other key words to look for:

God as Father	over 100 times
Eternal life	35 times
Witness	21 times
Love	20 times

STATISTICS OF JOHN'S GOSPEL
- 21 chapters
- 879 verses
- 19,099 words

CHAPTER BY CHAPTER

One way of viewing John's Gospel is to note (in each chapter) the portrayal of one special aspect of the work or character of Jesus.

Chapter	Character/work of Jesus	Reference in John
1	Son of God	1:1-14
2	Son of Man	2:1-11
3	Divine Teacher	3:3-21
4	Soul-winner	4:4-34
5	Great Healer	5:1-9
6	Bread of Life	6:25-59
7	Water of Life	7:37-39
8	Defender of the Weak	8:1-11
9	Light of the World	9:1-41
10	Good Shepherd	10:1-18
11	Prince of Life	11:1-44
12	King	12:12-16
13	Servant	13:1-17
14	Consoler	14:1-3
15	True Vine	15:1-16
16	Giver of the Holy Spirit	16:1-15
17	Great Intercessor	17:1-26
18	Model Sufferer	18:1-11
19	Uplifted Savior	19:16-19
20	Conqueror of Death	20:1-31
21	Restorer of the Penitent	21:1-19

KEY VERSE

The most preached-on and best-known verse in the Bible is John 3:16:

"For God so loved the world that he gave his one and only Son, that whoever believes in him shall not perish but have eternal life."

WHAT TO LOOK FOR IN JOHN'S GOSPEL

LOOK FOR DISTINCT FEATURES IN JOHN'S GOSPEL
One of the features of John's Gospel is its use of irony.
Also, throughout this Gospel people say and do things which
have a deeper significance than was realized at the time.

- God's own Son is put to death by God's own people.
- Jesus' shameful death on the cross reveals the glory of
  both the Father and the Son.

LENGTHY SERMONS REPLACE BRIEF SAYINGS
The other Gospels concentrate more on the brief sayings
and stories of Jesus, whereas John records longer sections of
teaching.

These discourses fall into two groups:

a. Jesus' public instruction to the world: 1–12
b. Jesus' private teaching to his disciples: 13–16

These discourses take up 41% of John's Gospel: 357 verses
out of 879 verses.

8

WHAT IS UNIQUE IN JOHN'S GOSPEL?
In addition to the twelve discourses which only appear in
John's Gospel, John alone records:

1. The last witness of John the Baptist	3:23-30
2. The anointing of Jesus at Bethany	12:1-11
3. Jesus' high priestly prayer	Chapter 17
4. Meeting Jesus' disciples at the sea of Galilee	Chapter 21
5. Six miracles.	See pages 18–19

DISCOURSES IN JOHN'S GOSPEL

No. of discourse	Topic of discourse	John
1.	Spiritual new birth	3:1-21
2.	Eternal life	4:4-26
3.	The source of eternal life and its witness	5:19-47
4.	The true Bread of Life	6:26-59
5.	The Source of Truth	7:14-29
6.	The Light of the World	8:12-20
7.	The true Object of faith	8:21-30
8.	Spiritual freedom	8:31-59
9.	The Good Shepherd	10:1-21
10.	The unity of God	10:22-38
11.	The world's Redeemer	12:20-36
12.	Teaching in the upper room	13:31–16:33
	a. The impending separation	13:31–14:31
	b. Union with Jesus	15:1-27
	c. The Holy Spirit and the future	16:1-33

ANOTHER WAY TO SPLIT UP JOHN'S GOSPEL

John's Gospel can be divided in numerous helpful ways. Before studying each chapter in detail, it's a good idea to read through the Gospel at one sittting.

The prelude	1:1-51
The book of signs	2:1–12:50
The book of passion	13:1–19:42
The resurrection and the epilogue	20:1–21:25

JESUS, THE SON OF GOD

READ JOHN'S GOSPEL
chapter 1

THE DISTINCTIVENESS OF JOHN'S GOSPEL

The opening fourteen verses of John's Gospel are among the profoundest words in the Bible. They have never been fully fathomed.

These verses teach that:
- the "Word of God" is active and living.
- the "Word of God" is Jesus.

William Temple

"The point of vital importance is the utterance of the Divine Word to the soul, the self-communication of the Father to his children. The Fourth Gospel is written with full consciousness of that truth." *William Temple*

WHAT DOES "THE WORD" MEAN?

"In the beginning was the Word, and the Word was with God, and the Word was God." *1:1*

- Jesus is spoken of as "the Word".
- "The Word" expresses the way in which the Creator God reveals himself to us, his creatures.
- All of the Wisdom behind the universe embodies itself in Jesus, the "Word."
- To the Jews, "the Word" meant the revelation of God's character. They knew that this was revealed to people in the pages of the Old Testament.
- Long before Jesus became a human, he existed. "In the beginning was the Word."
  "If God created 'in the beginning,' Genesis 1:1, then the uncreated Son was 'in the beginning.'" *A.B. Cundall*

ANDREW

"Andrew, Simon Peter's brother, was one of the two who had heard John the Baptist's words and had followed Jesus." *1:40*

Andrew in John's Gospel

• Andrew was hungry for the truth	*1:35-37*
• Andrew wanted to learn from Jesus	*1:38-39*
• Andrew brought his brother to Jesus	*1:41-42*
• Andrew had an eye for small things	*6:8-9*
• Andrew was chosen by Jesus and chose to stay with him	*6:66-70*
• Andrew was concerned about unbelievers	*12:20-22*

JESUS IS THE SON OF GOD

"Then Nathaniel declared, 'Rabbi, you are the Son of God, you are the King of Israel.'" *1:49*

John shows that Nathaniel acknowledged that Jesus, from the beginning of his ministry, was the Son of God.

Jesus, the Son of God, in John 1

• "The Word became flesh and made his dwelling among us. We have seen his glory, the glory of the One and Only, who came from the Father, full of grace and truth." *1:14*
• "No one has ever seen God, but God the One and Only, who is at the Father's side, has made him known." *1:18*
• [John the Baptist said:] "I have seen and I testify that this is the Son of God." *1:34*

MINI BIBLE STUDY

In addition to chapter one, the following two verses most clearly state that Jesus is the Son of God: John 3:16 and John 20:31.

At the end of Jesus' ministry this title, "Son of God," was used to taunt Jesus. See Matthew 27:40 and John 19:7.

JESUS, THE SON OF MAN

READ JOHN'S GOSPEL
chapter 2

JESUS GOES TO A WEDDING: JOHN 2:1-11

This event illustrates the humanity of Jesus. Jesus, as a guest at a wedding, mixed socially with other people.

JOHN SHOWS JESUS TO BE HUMAN

Jesus, like any other human being, was sometimes tired and in need of rest.

> "Jacob's well was there, and Jesus, tired as he was from the journey, sat down by the well." *4:6*

MINI BIBLE STUDY

Key references in John's Gospel reveal the humanity of Jesus.

John 1:14	John 5:27
John 11:35	John 13:31

MORE THAN THE SON OF MAN

The wedding at Cana reveals that Jesus was more than a mere man. He performed "signs." *2:11*

John never uses the word "miracles" but calls these miraculous events "signs."

SIGNS

- Signs do not concentrate on the wonder of the extraordinary event but emphasize its significance.
- John's use of "sign" [NIV "miraculous sign"] is also found in 4:54; 6:14; 9:16; 11:47.
- The twofold purpose of these "signs" is stated in 1:11:
  1. "He thus revealed his glory,
  2. and his disciples put their faith in him."

- The arrival of Jesus as the Son of God and as the Son of Man was one stupendous sign of God's glory.

  "The Word became flesh and made his dwelling among us. We have seen his glory the glory of the One and Only, who came from the Father, full of grace and truth." *1:14*

JESUS' MOMENT

When Jesus told his mother, "My time has not yet come," (*2:4*) he was showing that he was conscious of his divine mission. Here, and elsewhere, we see how aware he was that he was moving towards his special destiny:

a. "Therefore Jesus told them, 'The right time for me has not yet come.'" *7:6*
b. "I am not yet going up to this Feast, because for me the right time has not yet come." *7:8*
c. "At this time they tried to seize him, but no one laid a hand on him, because his time had not yet come.' *7:30*
d. "Yet no one seized him, because his time had not yet come." *8:20*

MINI BIBLE STUDY

Note when Jesus said that his time had come.

John 12:23	John 12:27
John 13:1	John 16:32
John 17:1	

JESUS CLEARS THE TEMPLE: JOHN 2:12-25

John presents another sign. Jesus now symbolically purifies the ways of temple worship.

Most people did not see this as a sign of the coming of the Messiah. Verse 18 states, "Then the Jews demanded of him, 'What miraculous sign can you show us to prove your authority to do all this?'" They forgot that this was a picture of the Lord of the Temple suddenly coming to his Temple. *See Malachi 3:1-3.* However, John records that the significance of this "sign" was not lost on Jesus' disciples. They recalled Psalm 69:9: "His disciples remembered that it is written, 'Zeal for your house will consume me.'" *2:17*

JESUS, THE DIVINE TEACHER

READ JOHN'S GOSPEL
chapter 3

A RELIGIOUS TEACHER VISITS THE DIVINE TEACHER

- The divine Teacher instructed Nicodemus, who was proud that he belonged to the top religious group in Israel. For Nicodemus was not just any old Pharisee: "He was a member of the Jewish ruling council." *3:1*
- Nicodemus showed his lack of spiritual insight. *3:3*. He did, however, recognize that Jesus was a teacher empowered by God. "We know you are a teacher who has come from God." *3:2*

GROWTH IN FAITH

This is not the end of the story of Nicodemus. Note two other significant events: John 7:45-52; John 19:38-42.

MINI BIBLE STUDY

Jesus the divine Teacher
Matthew 4:23; 5:2; 7:29
Mark   6:34
Luke   4:15; 5:3
John   3:2; 7:14; 8:2

JOHN 3:16

The great truth that lay behind God's plan of salvation is clearly stated in this verse. "For God so loved the world . . John 3:16 is God's answer to:

Atheism,	by the affirmation	"God"
Agnosticism,	by the statement	"God so loved"
Deism,	by the declaration	"God gave"
Pantheism,	by proclaiming	"God so loved the world"
Skepticism,	by announcing	"but have eternal life"
Legalism,	by specifying	"whoever believes"
Naturalism,	by promising	"shall not perish"

JOHN 3:16 AS THE GREATEST STATEMENT EVER MADE

God	the greatest Lover
so loved	the greatest degree of love
the world	the greatest company of people
that he gave	the greatest act
his one and only Son	the greatest gift
that whoever	the greatest opportunity
believes	the greatest simplicity
in him	the greatest attraction
shall not perish	the greatest deliverance
but	the greatest difference
have	the greatest certainty
eternal life	the greatest possession

JOHN 3:16 EXPLAINED

For God;	the Lord of earth and heaven,
so loved;	and longed to see forgiven,
the world;	in sin and pleasure mad,
that he gave	the greatest gift he had
his one and only Son	to take our place,
that whoever	oh, what grace!
believes	placing simple trust
in him,	the Righteous and the Just,
shall not perish,	lost in sin,
but have eternal life	in him.

STUDY A THEME IN JOHN
1. WITNESSES TO JESUS: THE EVIDENCE

JOHN'S EVIDENCE

"Witness," in the courtroom sense, is a crucial theme in John's Gospel. John brings forward witness after witness to testify that Jesus is the Christ, the Son of God.

WITNESS NO 1.
JOHN THE BAPTIST

John's witness to Jesus is recorded in:

John 1:6-8,15,19-36

> "The next day John saw Jesus coming towards him and said, 'Look, the Lamb of God, who takes away the sin of the world!'" *1:29*

John 3:25-30

> "I am not the Christ but am sent ahead of him." *3:28*

John 5:33-36

> "John was a lamp that burned and gave light, and you chose for a time to enjoy his light. I have testimony weightier than that of John." *5:35-36*

WITNESS NO 2.
THE OLD TESTAMENT

John shows how the Old Testament was always looking forward to the coming of the Messiah.

John 1:45

> "Philip found Nathanael and told him, 'We have found the one Moses wrote about in the Law, and about whom the prophets also wrote – Jesus of Nazaareth, the son of Joseph.'" *1:45*

John 5:39,46-47

> "These are the Scriptures that testify about me." *5:39*

John 8:56

> "Your father Abraham rejoiced at the thought of seeing my day; he saw it and was glad." *8:56*

WITNESS NO 3.
PEOPLE WHO MET JESUS
John 4:29,39
> "Come, see a man who told me everything I ever did. Could this be the Christ?" *4:29*

John 9:13-33,38
> "Nobody has ever heard of opening the eyes of a man born blind. If this man were not from God, he could do nothing." *9:32-33*

John 11:27
> "'Yes, Lord,' she [Martha] told him [Jesus], 'I believe that you are the Christ, the Son of God, who was to come into the world.'" *11:27*

WITNESS NO 4.
THE APOSTLES
John 1:41-46,49
John 15:27
> "And you also must testify, for you have been with me from the beginning." *15:27*

John 20:24-25,28

WITNESS NO 5.
THE FATHER
John 5:31-32,37
John 8:18,50,54
> "I am one who testifies for myself; my other witness is the Father, who sent me." *8:18*

John 12:27-28

WITNESS NO 6.
THE HOLY SPIRIT
John 14:26
John 15:26
> "When the Counselor comes, whom I will send to you from the Father, the Spirit of truth who goes out from the Father, he will testify about me." *15:26*

John 16:12-15

WITNESS NO 7.
THE DEEDS OF JESUS
John 2:11,23
John 5:36
John 9:3,31-33
John 10:25,37-38
> "The miracles I do in my Father's name speak for me." *10:25*

John 11:4,42,45
John 14:11
John 20:30-31

WITNESS NO 8. JESUS' CLAIMS ABOUT HIMSELF
See pages 36–37

STUDY A THEME IN JOHN
2. WITNESSES TO JESUS: THE VERDICT

JESUS DIVIDED PEOPLE
In John's Gospel, whenever the reaction to Jesus' words or deeds is recorded, there is a split decision. Some believed. Some didn't believe. "Thus the people were divided because of Jesus." 7:43

1. THE VERDICT OF THE PEOPLE WHO REJECTED JESUS
John 1:10-11
John 3:11
John 4:48
John 5:43
John 6:36,64,66
John 12:37,47-48
> "Even after Jesus had done all these miraculous signs in their presence, they still would not believe in him." *12:37*

John 15:19,24

2. THE REASONS GIVEN FOR REJECTING JESUS
John 3:19-21
> "This is the verdict: Light has come into the world, but men loved darkness instead of light because their deeds were evil." *3.19*

John 5:44
John 6:37,44,65
John 8:43-47
John 9:39-41
John 12:37-43
John 18:37

3. THE VERDICT OF THOSE WHO ACCEPTED JESUS

a. Those who accepted Jesus by seeing and listening to him

John 1:14

John 6:40,45

> "For my Father's will is that everyone who looks to the Son and believes in him shall have eternal life, and I will raise him up at the last day." *6:40*

John 10:3,16,27

John 12:45,47

John 14:9

John 18:37

b. Those who accepted Jesus by believing in him

John 1:7,12

John 2:11,22

John 3:16,18

John 5:24

> "I tell you the truth, whoever hears my word and believes him who sent me has eternal life and will not be condemned; he has crossed over from death to life." *5:24*

John 6:29,47

John 8:24

John 9:35-38

John 11:25-27,40

John 13:19

John 14:1,11

John 16:27,30

John 17:8

John 20:8,29,31

c. Those who accepted Jesus by coming to know him and who he is

John 6:69

John 7:17

John 8:19

John 10:14

John 14:7,9

John 17:3,25

> "Now this is eternal life: that they may know you, the only true God, and Jesus Christ, whom you have sent." *17:3*

For these people this meant:

a. living in the light
   John 1:4-5,9; 3:19-21; 8:12; 9:39; 11:9; 12:35-36,46

b. learning the truth
   John 1:14, 17; 4:23-24; 8:32; 14:6; 17:17; 18:37

d. Those who accepted Jesus by loving Christ and one another and obeying his words

John 7:17

John 13:34-35

> "A new command I give you: Love one another. As I have loved you, so you must love one another." *13:34*

John 14:15,21-24

John 15:9-10,12

John 21:15-17

For these people this meant abiding in Jesus:

John 15:1-10.

JESUS, THE SOUL-WINNER

READ JOHN'S GOSPEL
chapter 4

PERSONAL EVANGELISM

This chapter is often used to teach people how to lead someone to trust Jesus. Jesus leads this outcast Samaritan woman into the light.

MINI BIBLE STUDY

Other useful Bible references in this work.
[The numbers correspond to the numbers on the opposite page. The number "2" (reference Matthew 5:47), is about "Speak to the non-Christian with respect …"

- 2. Matthew 5:47
- 3. Acts 17:22-23, 28
- 4. Romans 6:23
- 5. John 3:8
- 6. Psalm 107:9
- 7. Luke 19:18; Matthew 19:21
- 8. 2 Corinthians 6:2; 1 Timothy 6:20
- 10. Acts 8:35
- 11. Matthew 9:29; Acts 8:36-38

KEY VERSE

"The fruit of the righteous is a tree of life, and he who wins souls is wise." *Proverbs 11:30*

GUIDELINES FOR INTRODUCING A PERSON TO JESUS

Thought/action required	Verse in John 4
1. Go to where non-Christians can be found.	"He had to go through Samaria." *(4)*
2. Speak to the non-Christian with respect and not in a patronizing or superior way.	"Jesus said to her, 'Will you give me a drink?'" *(7)*
3. Begin where the non-Christian is and any need that you are me aware of.	"Jesus answered her, 'If you knew the gift of God and who it is that asks you for a drink you would have asked him and he would have given you living water.'" *(10)*
4. Speak about God's gift.	
5. Use illustrations from everyday life.	*(10-12)*
6. Be satisfying and relevant.	"Whoever drinks of the water I give him will never thirst." *(3)*
7. Give non-Christians a chance to be truthful about sin.	"He told her, 'Go, call your husband and come back.'" *(16)*
8. Avoid being sidetracked by a change of topic.	*(19-21)*
9. Distinguish between a phoney question and a genuine question.	"The woman said, 'I know that Messiah' (called Christ) 'is coming. When he comes, he will explain everything to us.'" *(25)*
10. Answer questions with truths about Jesus.	"Then Jesus declared, 'I who speak to you am he.'" *(26)*
11. Don't be scared of potential results.	*(29-30)*
12. Encourage the new Christian to work for Jesus.	"Many of the Samaritans from that town believed in him [Jesus] because of the woman's testimony, 'He told me everything I ever did.'" *(39)*
13. Make introducing people to Jesus a top priority.	"'My food,' said Jesus, 'is to do the will of him who sent me and to finish his work.... Look at the fields! They are ripe for harvest.'" *(34-35)*

JESUS, THE GREAT HEALER

READ JOHN'S GOSPEL
chapter 5

JOHN 5:1-9
Points of interest to note:

- Jesus' concern for the ill.
- Jesus' power over illness.
- Jesus felt no one was beyond help.
- Jesus' instant healing.

"TO JERUSALEM FOR A FEAST OF THE JEWS"
All Jewish males were required to come to Jerusalem for three festivals:

- The Festival of Passover and Unleavened Bread
- The Festival of Pentecost (also called the Festival of Harvest or the Festival of Weeks)
- The Festival of Shelters

It is not clear which feast is meant here.

JESUS' BOLD CLAIMS ABOUT HIMSELF

Jesus claimed to be equal with God	"He was even calling God his own Father, making himself equal with God." *5:18*
Jesus claimed to give eternal life	"I tell you the truth, whoever hears my word and believes him who sent me has eternal life and will not be condemned; he has crossed over from death to life." *5:24*
Jesus claimed to be the source of life	"For as the Father has life in himself, so he has granted the Son to have life in himself" *5:26*
Jesus claimed to judge sin	"And he [God the Father] has given him [Jesus] authority to judge because he is the Son of Man." *5:27*

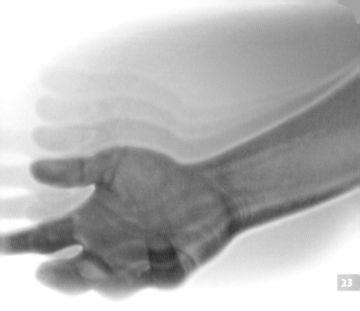

MINI BIBLE STUDY
John the Baptist's ministry confirms Jesus' claim to be divine: John 8:33-35

Compare

John 5:31	John 8:13-14
John 5:32	John 8:18
John 5:36	John 10:25,38; 14:11; 15:24; 1 John 5:9
John 5:37	Deuteronomy 4:12; John 1:18; 8:18; 1 Timothy 1:17
John 5:38	1 John 2:14
John 5:46	Genesis 3:15; Deuteronomy 18:15, 18; Luke 24:27,44; Acts 26:22,23
John 5:47	Luke 16:31

STUDY A THEME IN JOHN
3. MIRACLES

ONLY 8 MIRACLES
John only records eight out of the 35 miracles of Jesus described in the Gospels. Six out of these eight are unique to John's Gospel.

THE PURPOSE OF JOHN'S MIRACLES
The miracles which John, the eyewitness, chose to record in his Gospel were carefully selected. In all eight miracles or miraculous signs, as John preferred to call them, Jesus is seen as the Son of God. In addition to this each miracle had something special to reveal.

Miracles in John's Gospel		
	Teaching purpose of miracle	Reference in John
1. Turning water into wine	To reveal the glory of Jesus	2:1-11
2. Official's son healed	Faith is required "The man took Jesus at his word." *4:50*	4:46-54
3. Lame man healed	Power for true life comes from Jesus	5:1-9
4. Feeding of 5,000	Jesus gives spiritual food	6:1-14
5. Walking on water	Jesus' power to help and guide	6:16-21
6. Blind man healed	Jesus delivers from spiritual darkness	9:1-41
7. Lazarus raised	Victory of Jesus' life over death	11:1-44
8. The catch of fish	Jesus' abundant provision and encouragement	21:1-14

WHICH ARE THE SIX MIRACLES UNIQUE TO JOHN?
The feeding of the 5,000 and Jesus walking on water are the only two miracles which are not unique to John.

The feeding of the 5,000 is the only miracle to appear in all four Gospels. The account of Jesus walking on the water is told in Matthew and Mark, as well as in John.

OTHER SIGNS OF JESUS' DIVINITY IN JOHN'S GOSPEL

1. Escaping death

Jesus, somehow, managed to walk through the middle of the Jews, just as they "picked up stones to stone him." *See 8:57-59.*

2. Defeating death

- The resurrection of Jesus is usually thought of as the greatest miraculous event in the Gospel.
- This, as it were, set the seal of God's approval on his work of redeeming the world. Because Jesus was sinless, he could not remain dead, since death is the punishment for sin. Therefore God raised him from the dead. *20:1-12*
- Jesus passed through locked doors to reassure his disciples that his resurrection was true. *20:19*

Augustine on miracles

"I never have any difficulties in believing in miracles, since I experienced the miracle of a change in my own heart."
Augustine of Hippo

JESUS, THE BREAD OF LIFE

READ JOHN'S GOSPEL
chapter 6

"I AM THE BREAD OF LIFE"

Without the Bread of Life (Jesus) our souls would die of hunger. Jesus, himself, said:

> "I am the bread of life. He who comes to me will never go hungry, and he who believes in me will never be thirsty." *6:35*

OTHER SPIRITUAL FOOD

One of the re-occurring themes of the Bible is the importance of nourishment to strengthen our spiritual selves.

Eat what is good	"Why spend money on what is not bread, and your labor on what does not satisfy? Listen, listen to me, and eat what is good, and your soul will delight in the richest of fare." *Isaiah 55:2*
Feed with understanding	"Then I will give you shepherds after my own heart, who will lead you with knowledge and understanding." *Jeremiah 3.15*
Living bread	"I am the living bread that came down from heaven. If anyone eats of this bread, he will live forever. This bread is my flesh, which I will give for the life of the world." *John 6:51*
Spiritual food	"They all ate the same spiritual food." *1 Corinthians 10:3*
Spiritual drink	"… and drank the same spiritual drink, for they drank from the spiritual rock that accompanied them, and that rock was Christ." *1 Corinthians 10:4*

MANY DISCIPLES DESERT JESUS

"From this time many of his [Jesus'] disciples turned back and no longer followed him." *6:66*

WHY DID THEY LEAVE?

Because: "many of his disciples said, 'This is a hard teaching.'" *6:60*

In the ancient world the sacrifice of animals and the eating of sacrificed animals was common so Jesus' words were not hard to understand, but they were hard to accept. Jesus had just said, "Unless you can eat the flesh of the Son of Man and drink his blood, you have no life in you." *6:53*

Jesus is saying that his death on the cross as God's sacrifice has to be accepted and appropriated by faith. Individuals must feed their hearts, minds and spirits on the words and life of Jesus. Only then can one receive eternal life.

That was too difficult a saying for many of Jesus' followers who had no more than a loose commitment to him.

ONE WORSE THAN A DESERTER

- Judas was one of "the Twelve." *6:70*
- Surely nobody from within the specially chosen group of twelve apostles would desert Jesus, let alone betray him?
- Jesus described the traitor Judas as "a devil!" *6:70*
- Judas, "who … was later to betray him [Jesus]" *6:71*, is here labeled as the one who opposed Jesus in the spirit of Satan.

JESUS, THE WATER OF LIFE

READ JOHN'S GOSPEL
chapter 7

SATISFYING SPIRITUAL THIRST

Jesus claims to quench the thirst of the most parched soul.

> "On the last and greatest day of the Feast, Jesus stood and said in a loud voice, 'If anyone is thirsty, let him come to me and drink.'" *John 7:37*

"ON THE LAST AND GREATEST DAY OF THE FEAST"

1. The Feast

This was the "Feast of Tabernacles" *7:2*

It was a thanksgiving for harvest, held in September/October. Booths or tents made from leafy branches were set up all over Jerusalem. Pilgrims and the inhabitants of Jerusalem moved into these simple huts for the seven days of the feast. Hence the other name for this feast is the "Feast of Booths" or "Feast of Shelters".

Pilgrims from all over the world came to Jerusalem for this great Jewish festival.

> "Celebrate the Feast of Harvest with the firstfruits of the crops you sow in your field." *Exodus 23:16*

2. Last and greatest day

On the last day of this feast water from the pool of Siloam was offered in the Temple. This symbolic pouring out of water was appropriate since everyone was looking forward to God's provision of rain at the end of the long summer drought.

3. "Jesus stood" *7:37*

Rabbis and teachers usually sat when they taught. But on this occasion Jesus stood up to draw attention to his special message.

4. "Come to me and drink" *7:37*

Thirsty souls were invited by Jesus to "drink," thus finding lasting refreshment through faith in him.

In this dramatic way Jesus was saying that spiritual satisfaction was not brought by the Jewish faith, but by Jesus himself through the gift of the Spirit. *See verse 38.*

28

LIVING WATER

The Bible frequently pictures spiritual life as water.

• Jesus is the source of this living water

> "Jesus answered her [the Samaritan woman], 'If you knew the gift of God and who it is that asks you for a drink, you would have asked him and he would have given you living water.'" *John 4:10*

• This living water reaches our deepest needs. Jesus said:

> "Whoever believes in me, as the Scripture has said, streams of living water will flow from within him." *John 7:38*

• This living water is like a spring which never dries up:

> "For the Lamb at the center of the throne will be their shepherd; he will lead them to springs of living water." *Revelation 7:17*

• This living water produces a fruitful life:

> "On each side of the river stood the tree of life, bearing twelve crops of fruit, yielding its fruit every month. And the leaves of the tree are for the healing of the nations." *Revelation 22:2*

STUDY A THEME IN JOHN
4. SYMBOLS AND WORDS USED BY JOHN

The power of Christ strikingly pictured

"The four Gospels all had the same purpose: to point out Christ. The first three Gospels show his body, so to speak, but John shows his soul. For this reason I usually say that this Gospel is a key to understanding the rest; for whoever understands the power of Christ strikingly pictured here will then profit by reading what the others tell about the Redeemer who appeared." *John Calvin*

JOHN'S USE OF SYMBOLISM
• John's language is richly symbolic.
• He uses symbolism more than the other three Gospel writers put together.
• Symbols enabled John to present Jesus in an arresting and powerful way. He gives ordinary words deep theological significance. Often Jesus uses these symbolic words again and again.

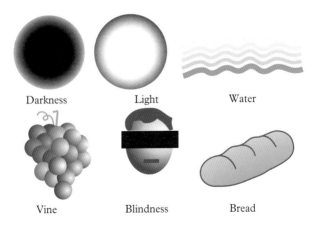

Darkness   Light   Water

Vine   Blindness   Bread

TEN EVERYDAY WORDS WITH DEEPER LAYERS OF MEANING WHEN USED BY JOHN IN HIS GOSPEL

Word used	Meaning of word	Reference in John
1. Belief	Active trust	3:16,18; 8:31-32
2. Death	Separation from God	5:24
3. Glory	God's splendor and power	1:14; 17:4-5
4. Hate	Implacable opposition to Jesus	3:20; 15:18-25
5. Knowledge	Personal experience of Jesus	8:31-32; 10:4-15
6. Eternal life	God's life in a person beginning now and continuing after death	3:15-36; 5:21-26
7. Love	Caring deeply for God and people	3:16; 15:9-13
8. Truth	Reality in the eyes of God	8:31-32
9. Word	Source of divine revelation	1:1-14
10. Freedom	Freedom from sin and therefore liberty to do God's will	8:32, 36

SIX SYMBOLIC WORDS USED BY JOHN IN HIS GOSPEL

Word used symbolically	Meaning of word	Reference in John
1. Darkness	Sin and the domination of evil	3:19; 8:12
2. Light	Spiritual understanding "This is the verdict: Light has come into the world, but men loved darkness instead of light because their deeds were evil." *3:19*	1:4-9; 3:19-21
3. Water	Spiritual life	7:37-39
4. Vine	Abiding in Jesus	15:1-11
5. Blindness	Lack of spiritual understanding	9:25
6. Bread	Spiritual food	6:33-51

JESUS, THE DEFENDER OF THE WEAK

READ JOHN'S GOSPEL 8:1-59

IS JOHN 7:53–8:11 IN THE BIBLE OR NOT?

This passage of the Bible is not found in the oldest manuscripts of the Bible. Some Bibles have therefore put it in brackets, or even left it out.

The NIV has this note: "The earliest and most reliable manuscripts and other ancient witnesses do not have John 7:53–8:11." But Papias, who lived soon after A.D. 100 does refer to this story

"A WOMAN CAUGHT IN ADULTERY" *verse 3*

This is one of the most telling incidents in the Gospels of Jesus' compassion for a sinner.

1. Should the woman be stoned?

"In the Law Moses commanded us to stone such women. Now what do you say?" *8:5*
Leviticus 20:10 stipulates that death should be the penalty for adultery. But Deuteronomy 22:22 adds that the man had to be stoned as well. The teachers of the law and the Pharisees had allowed the man to go free.

2. A trap

"They were using this question as a trap, in order to have a basis for accusing him." *8:6*
If Jesus had said that the woman should be stoned he would have been acting without mercy and would also have been defending the Romans, who did not allow the Jews to carry out the death penalty. *See John 18:31*

If Jesus had said she should not be stoned, he would have been accused of breaking the Jewish law and condoning serious sin.

3. Jesus' reply

"If any one of you is without sin, let him be the first to throw a stone at her." *8:7*
None of Jesus' accusers could claim to be without any sin so they, cowardly, crept away.

4. Condemnation for the sin, compassion for the sinner

Jesus did not condone this woman's adultery. He told her, "Go now and leave your life of sin." *8:11*
Jesus did not condemn her and instead offered her forgiveness. "Then neither do I condemn you." *8:11*

JOHN 8:12

"When Jesus spoke again to the people, he said, 'I am the light of the world. Whoever follows me will never walk in darkness, but will have the light of life.'" *8:12*

THE LIGHT OF THE WORLD

The scene is probably at the Feast of Tabernacles. This festival commemorated the pillar of fire in the wilderness.

"By day the Lord went ahead of them in a pillar of cloud to guide them on their way and by night in a pillar of fire to give them light, so that they could travel by day or night." *Exodus 13:21*

When darkness fell on the first day of the Feast of Tabernacles, four great candelabra were lit in the Temple Court of Women. This lit up the streets of Jerusalem, but then the light died away.

Jesus was taking up the symbolism of the candelabra when he said that he was "the light of life." *8:12*

"BLASPHEMY!" *John 8:58-59*

The Jews immediately saw that Jesus was applying the name "I AM," the name of God, to himself. He was daring to claim to be God.

Everybody knew what the punishment for such blasphemy was: it was stoning.

"'I tell you the truth,' Jesus answered, 'before Abraham was born, I am!' At this, they picked up stones to stone him ...'" *John 8:58-59*

JESUS, THE LIGHT OF THE WORLD

READ JOHN'S GOSPEL
chapter 9

A GRAPHIC ILLUSTRATION

Chapter 9 illustrates Jesus' proclamation in the previous chapter: "I am the light of the world." *8:12*

What Jesus does is inseparable from what he says. Jesus demonstrated this as he gave sight to someone who was born blind.

"The man they call Jesus made some mud and put it on my eyes. He told me to go to Siloam and wash. So I went and washed, and then I could see." *9:11*

WHO SINNED?

"As he [Jesus] went along, he saw a man blind from birth. His disciples asked him, 'Rabbi, who sinned, this man or his parents, that he was born blind?'" *9:1-2*

The Jews had this all worked out. The teaching they gave was similar to the advice Job received.

"You suffer now because you previously sinned."

"There is no death without sin, there is no suffering without iniquity."

But Jesus did not say that it was the blind man's fault, or the fault of his parents. Jesus rejected the suggestion that there was any direct link between this man's blindness and a specific sin.

"'Neither this man nor his parents sinned,' said Jesus, 'but this happened so that the work of God might be displayed in his life.'" *9:3*

PHYSICAL SIGHT AND SPIRITUAL SIGHT

"Jesus said, 'For judgment I have come into this world, so that the blind will see and those who see will become blind." *9:39*

The man Jesus had just cured received both physical sight and spiritual sight from Jesus. Jesus was taking the illustration of physical sight to tell the Jews that they were without spiritual sight.

JESUS BRINGS LIGHT

The imagery of God's light banishing darkness is used in a variety of ways in the Bible.

1. **From darkness to light**
   "The people walking in darkness have seen a great light; on those living in the land of the shadow of death a light has dawned." *Isaiah 9:2*

2. **Life and light**
   "In him [Jesus] was life, and that life was the light of men." *John 1:4*

3. **Light in our hearts**
   "For God, who said, 'Let light shine out of darkness,' made his light shine in our hearts to give us the light of the knowledge of the glory of God in the face of Christ." *2 Corinthians 4.6*

4. **When no earthly light will be needed**
   "The city does not need the sun or the moon to shine on it, for the glory of God gives it light, and the Lamb is its lamp." *Revelation 21:23*

JESUS, THE GOOD SHEPHERD

READ JOHN'S GOSPEL
chapter 10

"I AM THE GOOD SHEPHERD"

"I am the good shepherd. The good shepherd lays down his life for the sheep." *10:11*

This is the fourth of Jesus' "I am" sayings. A less well-known "I am" saying also comes in this chapter:

"I am the gate for the sheep." *10:7*

THE 7 "I AMS"

John's Gospel alone includes these, so-called, "I am" sayings of Jesus. On seven occasions through his Gospel John records that Jesus says, "I am." On each occasion Jesus said "I am" at a highly significant moment.

1. I AM the bread of life	6:35-40
2. I AM the light of the world	8:12-13
3. I AM the gate [door] for the sheep	10:7-10
4. I AM the good shepherd	10:11-18
5. I AM the resurrection and the life	11:17-27
6. I AM the way, truth and life	14:1-7
7. I AM the true vine	15:1-11

"I AM"

The phrase, "I am" points to the personal and distinctive name of God found in the Old Testament. "I am" speaks of the presence of God.

> "Moses said to God, 'Suppose I go to the Israelites and say to them, "The God of your fathers has sent me to you," and they ask me, "What is his name?" Then what shall I tell them?' God said to Moses, 'I AM WHO I AM. This is what you are to say to the Israelites: "I AM has sent me to you."'" *Exodus 3.13-14*

When Jesus used the phrase "I am," he was underlining his claim to be:

- pre-existent
- eternally God

THE CLAIMS OF THE "I AMS"

The "I am" sayings of Jesus spell out his claims.

- Each one says something distinctive about who Jesus is.
- Each one is linked to a promise about what Jesus is offering to someone who believes in him.

The claim	The promise
1. "I am the gate …	whoever enters through me will be saved." *10:9*
2. "I am the light of the world.	Whoever follows me will never walk in darkness, but will have the light of life." *8:12*

MINI BIBLE STUDY

Look up the other five "I am" sayings and note the claim and promise in each of them.

JESUS, THE PRINCE OF LIFE

READ JOHN'S GOSPEL
chapter 11

MARY, MARTHA AND LAZARUS

1. Mary
Mary, the sister of Martha and Lazarus, loved to sit at Jesus' feet and listen to his teaching. A short time before Jesus' death, Mary anointed his feet with expensive perfume, wiping his feet dry with her hair.
See John 12:1-8.

2. Martha
With her sister Mary, and brother, Lazarus, Martha often entertained Jesus in her home at Bethany, some two miles from Jerusalem. Martha once complained to Jesus that Mary just sat and listened to Jesus while she was left to do all the work. Jesus, however, replied that Mary had chosen what was better. *See Luke 10:38-42.*

3. Lazarus
Lazarus, brother of Mary and Martha, was loved by Jesus. When Lazarus died Jesus came to Lazarus' home in Bethany four days later. He wept with Lazarus' two grieving sisters and then brought him back to life explaining that he, Jesus, was the resurrection and the life. The Pharisees tried to kill Lazarus and Jesus because many people were putting their faith in Jesus as a result of this miracle.

"I AM THE RESURRECTION AND THE LIFE"
This is the fifth of Jesus' "I am" sayings. Jesus demonstrated his right to this title, "the resurrection and the life," by raising Lazarus from the dead. But Jesus was indicating that he gives even more than "resurrection and life." Because of who he is, final death was not a possibility for him.

- Jesus said, "I am … the life." *John 14:6*
- In his second sermon, Peter said, "You killed the author of life, but God raised him from the dead." *Acts 3:15*
- "And what we have said is even more clear if another priest like Melchizedek appears, one who has become a priest not on the basis of a regulation as to his ancestry but on the basis of the power of an indestructible life." *Hebrews 7:15-16*

"JESUS WEPT"

"Jesus wept" (*11:35*) is the shortest verse in the Bible.

1. Empathy with those who mourn a loved one

Jesus was deeply affected by the sight of mourning all around him. Jesus was to be greatly moved as he contemplated his own death. "Now my heart is troubled, and what shall I say? 'Father, save me from this hour?' No, it was for this very reason I came to this hour." *John 12:27*

As Jesus' face was bathed in tears the Jews saw how much he had loved Lazarus.

2. Anger against sin and death

"When Jesus saw her [Mary] weeping, and the Jews who had come along with her also weeping, he was deeply moved in his spirit, and troubled." *John 11.33*

It would appear that Jesus did not merely cry out of sympathy for Mary and Martha or because of his own loss of a much-loved friend, but his tears were also tears of anger. This is the meaning behind the Greek word used indicating he was deeply moved.

Jesus was probably revealing, by his tears, his anger against sin and death and against the unbelief of those around him who did not believe that he was "the resurrection and the life."

STUDY A THEME IN JOHN
5. JESUS AND THE FATHER

GOD THE SON

We are so familiar with the phrase that "Jesus, the Son of God," that we often forget its importance.

Jesus was no mere mortal. He was the Son of God. From this study in John's Gospel one can build their own picture of Jesus as the Son of God and of his inseparable links with the Father.

1. Jesus was involved in creation
a. John 1:1-18
  "Through him [Jesus] all things were made." *1:3*

2. Jesus came from heaven/the Father
a. John 3:13
b. John 3:31
c. John 7:29
d. John 8:42
e. John 16:28

3. The Father loves the Son
a. John 3:35
b. John 5:20

4. The Father gave his authority to Jesus
  John 3:35

5. The Father has entrusted judgment of people to Jesus
a. John 5:22-23
b. John 5:27

6. The Father and Jesus work together
a. John 5:19
b. John 5:30

7. Jesus came to do the Father's will
a. John 6:38
b. John 14:31

8. Jesus has a unique relationship with the Father
a. John 6:46
b. John 6:57
c. John 10:15
d. John 10:30
e. John 10:38
f. John 13:31-32
g. John 16:15
h. John 16:32
i. John 17:4-5

9. Jesus' teaching came from the Father
a. John 7:16-17
b. John 8:28-29
c. John 12:49-50

10. Jesus said the Father was greater than he was in his incarnate role
  John 14:28

11. Jesus prayed to the Father
a. John 11:41-42
b. John 17:1-26

12. Seeing Jesus is seeing the Father
a. John 12:44-45
   "When a man ... looks at me, he sees the one who sent me."
   John 12:44-45
b. John 14:7-11

13. Christians dwell in Jesus and the Father
a. John 14:20
b. John 17:21-23
   "May they also be in us so that the world may believe that you have sent me.'
   John 17:21

14. Jesus knew he would return to the Father
a. John 13:3
b. John 14:28
c. John 16:28
d. John 17:11
e. John 20:17

15. To hate Jesus is to hate the Father
   John 15:23

JESUS, THE KING

READ JOHN'S GOSPEL
chapter 12

ENTER THE KING

As Jesus rode into Jerusalem, he was acclaimed king of Israel by the crowd. The "great crowd" shouted: "Blessed is the King of Israel!" *12:13*

"HOSANNA"

"They took palm branches and went out to meet him [Jesus], shouting,

a. *'Hosanna!'*
b. 'Blessed is he who comes in the name of the Lord.'
c. 'Blessed is the King of Israel.'" *12:13*

    a. "Hosanna" is a Hebrew expression which means "save!" It had become an exclamation of praise.

    b. This is a quotation from Psalm 118:26.

    c. This is *not* a quotation from any psalm. It was added by the crowd. John is the only Gospel writer to record this. Here and throughout his record of Jesus' passion, John wanted to emphasize the kingship of Jesus.

JESUS AND THE DONKEY

"Jesus found a young *donkey* and sat upon it." *12:14*

Jesus rode into Jerusalem in this way in order to stir the faith of those who watched. But even his own disciples did not fully grasp what was being symbolized.

"At first his disciples did not understand all this. Only after Jesus was glorified did they realize that these things had been written about him and that they had done these things to him." *12:16*

More about the donkey

"Do not be afraid, O Daughter of Zion; see, your king is coming, seated on a donkey's colt." *12:15*

This quotation comes from Zechariah 9:9. Jesus entering the city not on a war-horse as if he were a conquering human king, but on a lowly animal of peace, a donkey, showed that this King had come to bring peace.

The next verse in Zechariah's prophecy goes on to say, "I will take away the chariots from Ephraim and the war-horses from Jerusalem, and the battle-bow will be broken. He will proclaim peace to the nations." *Zechariah 9:10*.

Jesus' entry was a triumphant one that heralded peace.

JESUS' KINGSHIP IN SCRIPTURE

Jesus' kingship was prophesied	"'The days are coming,' declares the Lord, 'when I will raise up to David a righteous Branch, a King who will reign wisely and do what is just and right in the land.'" *Jeremiah 23:5*
Nathanael acknowledged it	"Then Nathanael declared, 'Rabbi, you are the Son of God; you are the King of Israel.'" *John 1:49*
Jesus spoke about his kingship to Pilate	"'You are a king, then!' said Pilate. Jesus answered, 'You are right in saying I am a king. In fact, for this reason I was born, and for this I came into the world, to testify to the truth.'" *John 18:37*

JESUS, THE SERVANT

READ JOHN'S GOSPEL
chapter 13

FOOT-WASHING

"Jesus … began to wash his disciples' feet." *13.5*

Jesus assumed the place of a servant. Jesus, washing his disciples' feet, is a picture of his humble life of love.

JESUS AS SERVANT OF MEN AND WOMEN

Mark's Gospel most strongly emphasizes that Jesus lived, on our behalf, as a humble Servant in the service of God. However this theme is also apparent in many other places in the Bible. Matthew and Mark use nearly identical words in their key verse about Jesus being the Servant.

Matthew	Jesus came to serve and to give his life	"Just as the Son of Man did not come to be served, but to serve, and to give his life as a ransom for many." *Matthew 20:28*
Mark	He came to serve and to give his life	"For even the Son of Man did not come to be served, but to serve, and to give his live as a ransom for many." *Mark 10:45*
Luke	He came as one who serves	"For who is greater, the one who is at the table or the one who serves? Is it not the one who is at the table? But I am among you as one who serves." *Luke 22:27*
John	He did a servant's menial task	"So he [Jesus] got up from the meal, took off his outer clothing, and wrapped a towel round his waist. After that, he poured water into a basin and began to wash his disciples' feet, drying them with the towel that was wrapped around his waist." *John 13:4-5*
Paul	Jesus took on the servant's nature	"But made himself nothing, taking the very nature of a servant, being made in human likeness." *Philippians 2:7*

THE UPPER ROOM DISCOURSE

Unique to John's Gospel is the "Upper Room Discourse," *chapters 14–17.*

Over 90 per cent of John is unique to his Gospel. John does not contain a genealogy or any record of Jesus' birth, childhood, temptation, transfiguration, appointment of the disciples, nor any account of Jesus' parables, ascension, or great commission.

A MOST LOVING ACT

John 13:1–17:26 is an account of Jesus with his disciples in the upper room. This narrative provides:

• the longest account of what went on in the upper room
• but no actual description of the Lord's Supper itself.

The description of Jesus washing the disciples' feet illustrates Jesus' Servant attitude and overwhelming love, especially in view of the fact that even then, at such a crucial and dangerous time, the disciples were squabbling about prestige. *See Luke 22:24*

In the first 12 chapters of John's Gospel the word "love" occurs six times. In chapters 13–17 of John's Gospel the word "love" comes 31 times.

JESUS, THE CONSOLER

📖 **READ JOHN'S GOSPEL**
chapter 14

THE COMFORT OF JESUS

Jesus explains to his dumbfounded disciples that he is going to leave them. But he comforts them by saying that he will not leave them forever. He will return.

JOHN 14:1-3

"Do not let your hearts be troubled.
Trust in God;
trust also in me.
In my Father's house are many rooms …
I am going there to prepare a place for you …
I will come back
and take you to be with me
that you also may be where I am."
John 14:1-3

WHEN WILL THIS HAPPEN?

- Jesus will receive each of his followers at their death.
- Or, when he returns again. Whichever is the first to happen.

"SIXTH "I AM" SAYING

"Jesus answered, 'I am the way and the truth and the life. No one comes to the Father except through me.'" *John 14:6*

**Link between
the Old and the New**
"In the Old Testament the New is concealed,
in the New Testament the Old is revealed."
Augustine

ISAIAH AND JOHN

The New Testament and the Old Testament shed light on each other. The prophet Isaiah and the Gospel of John have special links.

JOHN AND ISAIAH

Topic	Read in Isaiah	Compare with John
1. Divine teaching	50:4-5	14:10; 17:6-8
2. Freedom from fear	41:10	14:1

"So do not fear, for I am with you; do not be dismayed, for I am your God. I will strengthen you and help you; I will uphold you with my righteous right hand." *Isaiah 41:10*
"Do not let your hearts be troubled. Trust in God; trust also in me." *John 14:1*

Topic	Read in Isaiah	Compare with John
3. The shepherd and the sheep	40:11	10:1-21
4. Water for the thirsty	41:18; 44:3; 48:21; 49:10; 55:1	4:13-14; 6:35; 7:37
5. The gift of the Spirit	59:21	14:26; 15:26; 16:13
6. Food for the hungry	49:10	6:35
7. The divine comforter	51:12	14:16
8. Worldwide salvation	45:22; 49:12; 56:7-8; 60:3	3:16; 4:21-24; 10:16
9. Sight for the blind	35:5	9:39
10. Freedom for the bound	61:1	8:36

JESUS, THE TRUE VINE

📖 **READ JOHN'S GOSPEL**
chapter 15

THE LAST "I AM" SAYING

"I am the true vine, and my Father is the gardener." *John 15:1*
This is the seventh and last of Jesus' "I am" sayings.

VINES IN THE BIBLE

In the Old Testament God' people, the Israelites, were
described as:

a vine:
"You brought a vine out of Egypt;
you drove out the nations and planted it."
Psalm 80:8

a vineyard:
"I will sing for the one I love
a song about his vineyard.
My loved one had a vineyard
on a fertile hillside. …
The vineyard of the Lord Almighty
is the house of Israel."
Isaiah 5:1,7

A SUGGESTIVE METAPHOR

The idea of the people of
Israel being like a vine indicates
that:

• they belonged to God
• they were tended by God
• they brought forth fruit for God.

John 15:1-17 shows that this is true for the followers
of Jesus. Note how this passage explains this fact, in great
detail.

BEING FRUITFUL

Five ways to become a fruitful vine:

1. Have constant contact with living water

"He is like a tree planted by streams of water, which yields its fruit in season and whose leaf does not wither. Whatever he does prospers." *Psalm 1:3*

2. Be attentive to God's Word

"But the one who received the seed that fell on good soil is the man who hears the word and understands it. He produces a crop, yielding a hundred, sixty or thirty times what was sown." *Matthew 13:23*

3. Kill off personal ambition and self-indulgence

"I tell you the truth, unless a kernel of wheat falls to the ground and dies, it remains only a single seed. But if it dies, it produces many seeds." *John 12:24*

4. Accept God's discipline

"He cuts off every branch in me that bears no fruit, while every branch that does bear fruit he prunes so that it will be even more fruitful." *John 15:2*

5. Keep in constant contact with Christ

"I am the vine; you are the branches. If a man remains in me and I in him, he will bear much fruit; apart from me you can do nothing." *John 15:5*

MINI BIBLE STUDY
Unfruitfulness

Here are five sobering aspects about a Christian who does not bear fruit.

Look up

1. God pronounces his judgment on such people	*Matthew 3:10*
2. Worldliness causes unfruitfulness	*Matthew 13:22*
3. Unfruitful Christians are a disappointment to Jesus	*Luke 13:6*
4. Thoughtless inactivity may lead to unfruitfulness	*Luke 19:20*
5. God does not ignore total and deliberate unfruitfulness	*Hebrews 6:8*

JESUS, GIVER OF THE HOLY SPIRIT

📖 **READ JOHN'S GOSPEL**
chapter 16

JESUS PREPARES THE DISCIPLES FOR HIS DEPARTURE

Jesus' disciples were upset to hear any talk about Jesus leaving them. But Jesus said that they would benefit if he went away.

> "It is *for your good* that I am going away. Unless I go away, the Counselor will not come to you; but if I go, I will send him to you." *John 16:7*

"THE COUNSELOR WILL NOT COME"

Jesus did not actually explain why the Holy Spirit would only come if he went away. But Jesus did explain that he had to die for the sins of the world before sending the Spirit.

> "By this he meant the Spirit, whom those who believed in him were later to receive. Up to that time the Spirit had not been given, since Jesus had not yet been glorified."
> *John 7.39*

"I WILL SEND HIM TO YOU"

The Holy Spirit is a *gift* from Jesus. This aspect is linked with faith in Jesus, as well as repentance and obedience.

> "Peter replied, 'Repent and be baptized, every one of you, in the name of Jesus Christ for the forgiveness of your sins. And you will receive the *gift* of the Holy Spirit.'" *Acts 2:38*

TAUGHT BY THE SPIRIT

> "But when he, the Spirit of truth, comes, he will guide you into all truth. He will not speak on his own; he will speak only what he hears, and he will tell you what is yet to come." *John 16:13*

The teaching ministry of the Holy Spirit:

- guided the disciples into all the truths about Jesus
- enabled them to write down, interpret and pass on the unique events relating to the life, death and resurrection of Jesus.

50

WHAT IS THE GOAL OF THE WORK OF THE HOLY SPIRIT?

To bring glory to Jesus.

> "He will bring glory to me …" *John 16:14*

HOW DOES THE HOLY SPIRIT BRING GLORY TO JESUS?

By never drawing attention to himself, but only to Jesus.

> "… by taking from what is mine and making it known to you." *John 16:14*

THE COUNSELOR

John uses the word "Counselor" to describe the work of the Holy Spirit. The Greek word for "Counselor" is *parakletos*, which usually means "advocate", someone who speaks on another's behalf, and who defends that person.

> "If anybody does sin, we have one who speaks to the Father in our defence ["an advocate" KJV] Jesus Christ, the Righteous One."

"Counselor" means:
• Advocate
• Someone called alongside to help
• Encourager
• Consoler

MINI BIBLE STUDY

See how you can benefit from the ministry of the Holy Spirit as you look up the word "Counselor" in John's Gospel.

John 14:16
John 14:26
John 15:26
John 16:7

STUDY A THEME IN JOHN
6. THE HOLY SPIRIT

JOHN'S GOSPEL AND THE HOLY SPIRIT
John has more teaching about the Holy Spirit than the other three Gospels. We are told that the Holy Spirit would replace Jesus when Jesus returned to heaven.

MAJOR BIBLE STUDY
Where to find teaching about the Holy Spirit in John
If you had never heard of the Holy Spirit before reading these two pages, you can learn about him from the following Bible references in John's Gospel. Try writing down your discoveries.

Seven aspects of the work of the Holy Spirit have been inserted already in this study.

John 1:32-33	
John 3:5-6,8,34	
John 4:23-24	
John 6:63	The Holy Spirit gives spiritual life
John 7:37-39	
John 14:16-17,25-26	
John 14:16	The Holy Spirit lives in Christians
John 14:26	The Holy Spirit teaches Christians
John 15:26	The Holy Spirit testifies about Jesus
John 16:7-15	
John 16:7-11	The Holy Spirit convicts us about sin
John 16:13	The Holy Spirit guides into truth
John 16:14	The Holy Spirit brings glory to Jesus
John 20:22	

THE HOLY SPIRIT ON A BROADER CANVAS

Here are some ways in which the rest of the New Testament outside John's Gospel teaches that the ministry of the Holy Spirit helps all Christians, everywhere, in every age.

14 more encouraging facets about the ministry of the Holy Spirit

1. The Holy Spirit sets God's seal on Christians	Ephesians 1:13-14
2. The Holy Spirit reveals God's love in Christians	Romans 5:3-5
3. The Holy Spirit, who fathoms God's depths, reveals God's purposes	1 Corinthians 2:10
4. The Holy Spirit fills Christians	Ephesians 5:18
5. The Holy Spirit guides Christians into godliness	Ezekiel 36:27
6. The Holy Spirit strengthens Christians	Acts 9:31
7. The Holy Spirit helps Christians in their weakness	Romans 8:26
8. The Holy Spirit prays for Christians	Romans 8:26-27
9. The Holy Spirit brings hope	Romans 15:13; Galatians 5:5
10. The Holy Spirit imparts assurance that Christians belong to God	1 John 4:13; Romans 8:9,14,16
11. The Holy Spirit enables Christians to witness	Acts 1:8; Luke 24:46-49
13. The Holy Spirit builds up the Christian church	Acts 9:31
14. The Holy Spirit directs Christians in their witness and service	Acts 13:2, 20:28

JESUS, THE GREAT INTERCESSOR

READ JOHN'S GOSPEL
chapter 17

FOUR RELATIONSHIPS

Chapter 17 of John's Gospel sets out some important teaching about the good news of the Christian faith. It can be traced through four relationships.

The relationship of the father and son	17:1-5
The relationship of the son to the disciples and the relationship of the disciples to the world	17:6-19
The relationship of the Son to future believers	17:20-26

JOHN'S GOSPEL AND JESUS AT PRAYER

John chapter 17 is the longest prayer of Jesus recorded in the New Testament. Before he returned to heaven Jesus prayed for his church and the followers he was leaving behind.

FOUR WAYS IN WHICH JESUS' PRAYED FOR OTHERS

1. Jesus prays for sinners
   a. "He bore the sin of many, and made intercession for the transgressors." *Isaiah 53:12*
   b. "Jesus said, 'Father, forgive them, for they do not know what they are doing.'" *Luke 23:34*

2. Jesus prays for weak followers
   "But I have prayed for you, Simon, that your faith may not fail. And when you have turned back, strengthen your brothers." *Luke 22:32*

3. Jesus prays for his church
   "I pray for them. I am not praying for the world, but for those you have given me, for they are yours." *John 17:9*

4. Jesus continues to pray for us
   a. "Christ Jesus ... is at the right hand of God ... interceding for us. "*Romans 8:34*
   b. "Therefore he is able to save completely those who come to God through him, because he always lives to intercede for them." *Hebrews 7:25*

MAJOR BIBLE STUDY

There are numerous links between John's Gospel and 1 John which require careful comparison.

20 topics in both John's Gospel and John's first letter

Topic	John's Gospel	John's first letter (1 John)
1. The Word	1:1	1:1
2. Jesus made known	1:14	1:2
3. Joy complete	15:11	1:4
4. Light	1:7-9	1:5
5. Keeping God's word	14:23	2:5
6. Abiding in Jesus	15:4,7	2:6,28
7. A new command	13:34	2:8
8. Light in darkness	1:5	2:8
9. No stumbling	11:10	2:10
10. Knowing God	17:3	2:13
11. Children of God	1:12	3:1
12. Seeing Jesus	17:24	3:2
13. The devil's work	8:44	3:8
14. Love one another	13:34	3:11
15. Hatred from the world	17:14	3:13
16. God's one and only son	3:16	4:9
17. God has never been seen	1:18	4:12
18. Born of God	1:13	5:1
19. Are written/I write these things	20:31	5:13
20. The true God	17:2-3	5:20

JESUS, THE MODEL SUFFERER

READ JOHN'S GOSPEL
chapter 18

THE CUP

"Jesus commanded Peter, 'Put your sword away! Shall I not drink the cup the Father has given me?'" *John 18:11*

Jesus shows that he is quite prepared to drink the *cup* of suffering which the Father has prepared for him. *The cup* refers to the suffering, isolation, and death that Jesus would have to endure to atone for the sins of the world. See Matthew 20:22; 26:39.

ANNAS AND CAIAPHAS: JOHN 18:13

Both Annas and Caiaphas had been high priests. Annas was Israel's high priest from A.D. 6 to 15 when he was deposed by Roman rulers.

Caiaphas, Annas's son-in-law, was appointed high priest from A.D. 18 to 36/37. According to Jewish law, the office of high priest was held for life. Many Jews, therefore, still considered Annas the high priest and still called him by that title. But although Annas retained much authority among the Jews, Caiaphas made the final decisions.

Both Caiaphas and Annas cared more about political ambition than about their responsibility to lead the people to God.

PILATE

"Pilate said, 'Take him yourselves and judge him by your own law.'" *John 18:31*

Pilate made four attempts to deal with Jesus.

1. He tried to put the responsibility on someone else.	18:31
2. He tried to find a way out by releasing Jesus.	18:39
3. He tried to compromise by having Jesus flogged rather than handing him over to die.	19:1-3
4. He tried a direct appeal to the accusers.	19:15

"I FIND NO BASIS FOR A CHARGE AGAINST HIM." *19:38*
That was Pilate's considered opinion. The Gospel writers emphasize that there was no question of Jesus being anything other than completely innocent of the trumped up charges levelled against him.

FIVE OTHER WITNESSES WHO SAID OF JESUS, "YOU ARE INNOCENT"

1. Judas	"I have betrayed *innocent* blood."	Matthew 27:4
2. Pilate's wife	"Don't have anything to do with that *innocent* man."	Matthew 27:19
3. Herod	Pilate said that Herod had sent Jesus back, as he had "done nothing to deserve death."	Luke 23:15
4. Criminal	"This man has done nothing wrong."	Luke 23:41
5. Centurion	"Surely this was a righteous man."	Luke 23:47

MINI BIBLE STUDY
Read through 1 Peter 2:20-24 and see how Peter came to understand Jesus' suffering.

JESUS, THE UPLIFTED SAVIOR

READ JOHN'S GOSPEL
chapter 19

WHY DID JESUS DIE?

It's amazing to see how many people fail completely to see the real purpose of Jesus' death. Yes …

- He was brave
- He forgave his executors
- He died as if he had been a martyr
- He cared for others as he died:
  the repentant thief *Luke 23:43*
  Mary his mother *19:26-27*
- He was a model of an innocent man holding up under injustice and unbelievably painful suffering.

But none of these positive things come close to being the right answer to the question: "Why did Jesus die?"

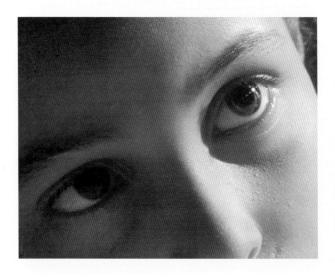

JOHN'S GOSPEL TELLS US WHY

More explicitly than the other Gospels, John shows us:

- why Jesus had to die, and
- the love that enabled him to do this.

1. Jesus is a Lamb

Why should John the Baptist say on seeing Jesus, "Look, the Lamb of God"? *John 1:29*

Nowhere else in the Bible, except in John 1:36, is the expression "Lamb of God" found. So what did John mean? John knew that Jesus was the one "who takes away the sin of the world!" (John 1:29). So John called Jesus "the Lamb of God." And all the people in the crowd knew the Old Testament passage:

"He was oppressed and afflicted, yet he did not open his mouth; he was led like a lamb to the slaughter, and as a sheep before her shearers is silent, so he did not open his mouth." *Isaiah 53:7*

The sacrifice of the lamb, Jesus, would atone for the sins of the world.

2. The love of Jesus

Jesus himself explained why he died and showed the love that lay behind his sacrifice for sin on the cross when he said to his disciples: "Greater love has no one than this, that he lay down his life for his friends." *John 15:13*

Jesus sacrificial death revealed the extent of his love for us.

MINI BIBLE STUDY

Observe further teaching John gives about Jesus' death.

	Look up in John
3. Jesus died [was lifted up] to "save" the world	*3:14-17; 8:28; 11:50-52; 12:24,27,32-34*
4. Jesus talked of "bread" [his body/ flesh/blood] giving life	*6:50-51,53-56*
5. Jesus predicted that he would rise again after he died	*2:19-22*
6. Jesus, the good shepherd, laid down his life for the sheep	*10:11,15,18*

JESUS, THE CONQUEROR OF DEATH

READ JOHN'S GOSPEL
chapter 20

JESUS DEFEATS DEATH

During his ministry Jesus revealed his power over death three times. He brought back to life:

1. A young girl	See Matthew 9:24-25
2. A grown up man, already in his coffin	See Luke 7:11-17
3. A friend, Lazarus, who had been dead for four days	See John 11:43-44

But in all these instances, the people died again.

JESUS COMES ALIVE AFTER DEATH – FOR EVER

John says that when he went into Jesus' tomb, he realized that the body was not there. "He saw and believed." *John 20:8*

Jesus had overcome death. Mary Magdalene also discovered this for herself. *John 20:18*

Later, the risen Lord Jesus was seen by all the apostles, except for Thomas and Judas Iscariot. *John 20:19-23*

Then he was seen by the ten apostles and by Thomas. *John 20:24-29*

DEATH HAS BEEN SWALLOWED UP

The apostle Paul's cardinal belief was in Jesus' resurrection.

• Death had now been defeated:
   "Death has been swallowed up in victory. Where, O death is your victory?"
   1 Corinthians 15:54-55

• With death overcome, Jesus was alive for ever. Paul's cry was:
   "Christ has indeed been raised from the dead."
   1 Corinthians 15:20

EVERLASTING LIFE

After his resurrection, Jesus' disciples came to understand his words to them during his lifetime. Now they could make sense of his teaching about "everlasting life."

To grumbling Jews, in the hearing of his disciples, Jesus had said:

> "He who believes [in Jesus and in God the Father] has everlasting life." *John 6:47*

The disciples began to realize that Jesus did not just offer life for the here and now, but for here and hereafter.

WHAT JESUS' RESURRECTION MEANT TO JOHN

The resurrection of Jesus is the climax to John's Gospel. After taking 29 verses to tell us how the disciples came to believe in Jesus' resurrection, John adds the conclusion to his Gospel:

> "Jesus did many other miraculous signs in the presence of his disciples, which are not recorded in this book. But these are written that you may believe that Jesus is the Christ, the Son of God, and that by believing you may have life in his name." *John 20:30-31*

JESUS' RESURRECTION AND BELIEF

In his first chapter John had stated Jesus' purpose in coming to earth.

> "So that through him all men might believe." *John 1:7*

John's aim was to draw the reader to believe in Jesus. This is stated categorically in John 20:30-31. Just to make sure no one would miss his message, John used the verb "believe" 98 times.

JESUS, THE RESTORER OF THE PENITENT

📖 **READ JOHN'S GOSPEL**
chapter 21

BREAKFAST WITH JESUS

After the miraculous catch of fish, John 21:1-14, seven of Jesus' disciples had a breakfast of roasted fish and bread with Jesus.

> "Jesus came, took the bread and gave it to them, and did the same with the fish." *John 21:13*

While this can hardly qualify as a commemoration of the Lord's Supper, it is an instructive picture of what every celebration of Jesus' death should be like. It is eating together in the presence of the risen Lord Jesus.

JESUS AND PETER

Jesus welcomed Peter and reinstated him.

> "Jesus said [to Peter], feed my sheep". *John 21:17*

Jesus said this three times, 21:15,16,17. This threefold commission can be seen as evidence that Peter had repented of his threefold denial of Jesus.
See John 18:15-18,25-27

PETER, THE PASTOR

These words of Jesus were not wasted on Peter for Peter, in turn, told elders in the church to be good spiritual shepherds.

> "To the elders among you, I appeal as a fellow-elder, a witness of Christ's sufferings and one who also will share in the glory to be revealed. Be shepherds of God's flock that is under your care."
> *1 Peter 5:1-2*

PETER'S DEATH

Jesus indicated "the kind of death by which Peter would glorify God." *John 21:19*

> "When you are old you will stretch out your hands, and someone else will dress you and lead you where you do not want to go." *John 1:18*

This was taken to mean that Peter would be crucified. Although Peter's death is not recorded in the Bible, he is thought to have been crucified upside down.

PETER'S PREACHING

Peter became the first Christian preacher in the early church. His message was clear:

> "Repent, then, and turn to God, so that your sins may be wiped out." *Acts 3:19*

KEY VERSES TO MEMORIZE FROM JOHN

GOD SO LOVED

"For God so loved the world that he gave his one and only Son, that whoever believes in him shall not perish but have eternal life." *3:16*

THAT YOU MAY BELIEVE

"Jesus did many other miraculous signs in the presence of his disciples, which are not recorded in this book. But these are written that you may believe that Jesus is the Christ, the Son of God, and that by believing you may have life in his name." *20:30-31*

CHILDREN OF GOD

"Yet to all who received him, to those who believed in his name, he gave the right to become children of God." *1:12*

THE GOOD SHEPHERD

"I am the good shepherd. The good shepherd lays down his life for the sheep." *10:11*